To Farah,

This Woman

Nancy Charley

Nancy Charley

THE
CONVERSATION
PAPERPRESS

First published 2012 by
THE CONVERSATION PAPERPRESS LTD.
Upper Roundell, Park Road, Faversham, Kent ME13 8ES, UK.
www.conversationpoetry.co.uk

ISBN 978-0-9563137-8-2

Printed and bound in the UK by
Lightning Source UK Ltd.

Cover design developed from 'Blanket', a painting by Haymanot Tesfa.

For Jeremy,
with thanks for the question...

This woman

was a river flowing
    through a parched landscape.

They walked upon her water,
    cleansed, bathed and drank.

They drifted with her current,
    navigating rapids.

A channel to new places
    to trade, travel, to meet, matter.

But when rainfall slackened
    they tried to dam her.

A muddied trickle. She limps
    from source to mouth.

This
woman,
one gritstone
in dry stone wall
(boundary marker).
No mortar, yet placed
so exactly that extraction
would precipitate a total coll-

apse.

This woman

        hides a child inside
who fears the bully's taunt *you're strange,*
can't find the right way to behave
to imitate the popular ones,
so learns to camouflage the wounds
from spiteful tongues, whilst staying dumb.

Though grown up she effuses love,
can laugh and smile quite easily,
relishes others' company,
has many who would call her friend,
the child can still play saboteur,
panic with fear, cry out in pain.

This woman

                is a whirlpool.
          Churning, turning, fluid mass,
          vortexing. Full of flood debris,
          fast-flowing. Caught in narrow
          straits. She can't race free.
Locate her heart or you
will be sucked in.

This woman

as a lake deep underground

is fed by river,
                 stream,
                         trickle
seeping
        through
                 cracks
                         and crevices.

Hidden, unfathomable,
        somehow unimaginable
                where stalactite and stalagmite
                        grow unobserved.

When rainfall's heavy
                waters rise
        and walkers feel paths cling,
  longing to pull them in.

Sometimes the lake sends out a song:
  Deep calls to deep –
                and those drawn
  to the sound seek out its source,

drink sustenance and pain.

Waters swirl, patterning earth's
   groans,
         shifts,
                suffering,

   and sporadically spout
                a geyser shout.

This woman

as an adder waking in the spring
knows she must feed, mate,
have offspring.

So does.

She becomes dull,

loses sight of where she's at
and irritable.

Do not manhandle.

She needs to shed this skin
for growth,
vibrant continuing.

This woman

        is a volcano,
dormant, adept at passivity,
seemingly undisturbed by grazing sheep,
mountain bikers, picnicking families.

Some venture to her rim
to fleetingly peer at what's within,
others armed with instruments
try to gauge her seismic strength.

Only the canny ones notice
the fresh activity – spurts of steam,
shudders deepening and lava seep
increased from trickle to stream.

But who has eyes to see?
Her core is pushing to erupt
and by lava rush, ash cloud dust
will wreck, reform her landscape.

This woman

as a river in flash flood
is dangerous to those

who underestimate the water's rise,
the hidden pull of swirling undercurrent.

Relentless roar, a boulder-juggling torrent
delighting in the flinging of detritus.

Manmade barriers will not be sufficient
to direct her flow,
                    impose past limits.

This woman

was a fertile field.
Yearly the farmer planted seed
and harvested good yield.

He cropped intensively,
applying fertilizer, pesticide,
monitoring obsessively,

till she could not sustain
his expectation, could not nurture
another year's grain.

A paltry harvest,
no rustling waves in summer breeze,
no golden gleam at sunset.

The farmer deserted,
left her stripped, whipped by storms.
She reverted

to squalid mire.
But nature heals. Grasses sprouted,
then meadow flowers

attracting bees and butterflies,
her hedgerow sheltering birds and mice.
A survivor, come back to life.

And those who chance upon her
stop,
gaze, restored to wonder.

This woman

> *is carbon, common stuff,*
> *found in great abundance.*

But is she graphite?

> *soft, opaque, lubricating,*
> *thermal insulating,*
> *electrical conductor,*
> *useful for writers.*

Or diamond?

> *stops electricity,*
> *conducts heat rapidly,*
> *abrasive, clearly lustrous,*
> *beautiful even when uncut.*

Hard to say?

> *one thing's for sure,*
> *each time you expire*
> *she's released more and more.*

This woman

        seems as a lake
whose tranquillity restores
all who gather at her shore.

Children splash in the shallows,
cause ripples tossing pebbles,
chase darting fish, hunt treasures.

Some sail across her surface,
flirt with breeze, enclosed by hull
or windsurfing dash, dance, race.

Some relax with rod and line,
sketchbook, camera, open gaze,
fishing peaceful memories.

She freezes in midwinter.
Some skate with grace, some bump, fall.
All test for thin-ice danger.

Swimmers outstrip with strong-arm
pace, but stretched limbs soon succumb,
lost to her caressing lap.

So few dare dive into her depths.

This woman

        as a sitar string
plays best when taut in true tension,

        too tight, becomes sharp,
makes sympathetic strings jangle,

        too slack, becomes flat,
and drones hum monotonously,

        tuned, flauntily sings
jaunty or haunting melodies.

Yet, she is fraying, under strain
on this sitar – no touch, no pluck

vibrates her to thrilling climax.
She fantasises she's restrung

on guitar, cello, violin,
or Celtic harp or tea-chest bass…

This woman

        as a kite, lives to fly,
      to dance in wind
    and flirt with sun,
       a silhouette against full moon.

When packed away is insignificant –
   flat, inert, tightly curled, struts removed.

      Once launched
   by one who didn't
      know how to wield her,
            yield her to the wind,
     she nose-
    dived, crash-
         landed,
     snapped.

She fell upon an expert whose restoring hands
mended, then sent her soaring.

His passion keeps her in the sky

    swirling

     whirling

      wild-flying

arms entwining

with her lines.

She dreams her lift will find him surfing waves.

This woman

> as a smock windmill
> would daily twist her cap
> to face her sails into the wind
> to drive her stones
> to grind the grain
> to sustain
> those in her community.

> Landmark of grace and beauty.

> Iconic still
> > but seasons turn,
> her form adorns a changed landscape.
> She's shifted gear – to educate,
> give inspiration, entertain.

This woman

is copper mixed with zinc
to form the alloy brass

which mimics gold,
is useful for locks and pans,
doorknobs and saxophones.

But she's increased the heat
(420°C).
Result: liquid zinc.

Her potential currently?
To transmit high voltage electricity.

This woman

     found equatorial living was not to her liking -
          no deviation in day and night,
               so little heat variation

          so drifted
        north, then south
     enchanted by the changing
       landscape, weather
        seasons, animals
          plants

but found she was still circling

   so launched herself

        into outer space

           for eccentric orbiting.

of dangerous dreams…
and delighting in the deluge
tossing colours to the wind
She's sitting at a rainbow's end,
if you like life as black and white.
so is uncomfortable company
She's elasticising boundaries,

(his arguments were unconvincing).
to discuss her motivation
a forensic psychologist onto their show
that Richard and Judy once brought
                            So much so

sinner with saviour.
such unorthodox behaviour mingles
She plays with fire, creates mosaics,
divert those with strict directions.
Her juggling balls and spinning plates

she's always sought to question and subvert.
(and though often been much too self-righteous)
Through the years she's taken different guises,

                plays the fool.

This woman

This woman

is a Henry Moore sculpture,
not cast in bronze
but carved
from stone or wood.

The raw material
taken, handled
until grain, veins, blemishes
are understood.

Imagination, skill, love
work on each feature,
countless hours
of penetrating labour

to find the finished form.
Strong, durable,
yet spaces   holes reveal
she's seductive,

vulnerable.
And though a sign says
Do Not Touch
who'll resist a caress, a hug.

This woman

        as a computer
stores countless possibilities,
permutations, probabilities.

Multimedia technology
programmed imaginatively,
rationally (but is emotive too!)

She processes, then presents
her findings accessibly
poetically, prophetically.

She networks place and people.
She's heading for the future
(though viruses can still shut her down).

This woman

        is an eagle,
exultant when soaring,
rejoicing in flight.

Cliff-high she built her eyrie,
brooded all her young.

Taught to feed, fly and hunt,
fledged, they have begun
discovering territories,
rising to new heights,

exultant when soaring,
rejoicing in flight.

This woman

is a polished oak bookcase, sensuous
to touch, run fingers round the whirling grain.

Her wood sourced for endurance, strength.
She's bespoke, dovetailed - no cheap flatpack.

And even if your fingers trail through dust
there's no denying her magnificence.

But the real treasure is within,
pick from a shelf and you'll discover

curtain making, driving lessons,
concreting foundations, tips on self-motivation,

coping with teething and stroppy teenagers,
the simple art of pleasing a man,

recipes for dinners in under 20 minutes,
for bread, jam, playdoh and birthday cakes,

theories on women and church through the
ages,
competence in differentiation and integration,

the complexities of being female,
how to spot a friend from a manipulator,

clinging to grace, surviving storms,
peaceful lakes, raging volcanoes.

You'll lose time engrossed in her stories and poems
longing to be the character she'd have you become.

This woman

one person   feminine

one life   multifaceted

unique   complex

sentient   sensuous

alive

27

Nancy Charley was born in 1963. She has had poems published in several anthologies and magazines. She is a spoken word artist and has performed her poetry at theatres, arts centres and pubs, for Human Rights, for new Writing Nights and for the sheer enjoyment. She loves to probe, to question and to tell stories. But most of all she loves being a woman.

Lightning Source UK Ltd.
Milton Keynes UK
UKOW050600170912

199133UK00002B/2/P